Excel for Beginners

A Quick, Comprehensive, and Step-by-Step Guide
to Learn Excel Fundamentals, Formulas, Functions,
Macros, Management, and Visualization of Data
with Practical Examples

Robert B. Klatt

ISBN-13: 979-8878767354

DEDICATION

To every one of my readers!

TABLE OF CONTENT

Introduction

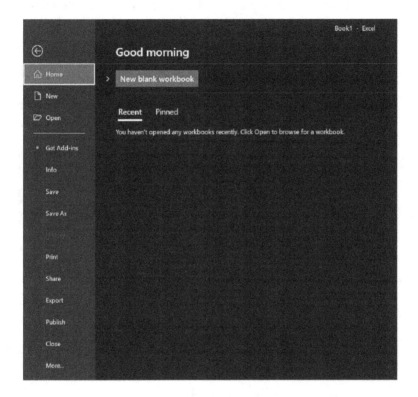

Microsoft Excel is a powerful and widely used spreadsheet program that has revolutionized the way we handle data and perform calculations. With its intuitive interface and extensive range of features, Excel has become an indispensable tool for businesses, students, and professionals across various industries.

In this introduction to Microsoft Excel, we will explore the basics of this software and its potential applications. Whether you're a beginner or have some prior experience with Excel, this guide will provide you with a solid foundation to navigate and utilize this versatile program effectively.

Excel allows you to organize, analyze, and visualize data in a structured and efficient manner. From creating simple tables to complex formulas and functions, Excel offers a wide range of tools to help you manipulate and interpret your data. You can perform calculations, generate charts, and create insightful reports with just a few clicks.

One of the key features of Excel is its ability to handle large amounts of data. Whether you're dealing with financial records, sales figures, or scientific data, Excel can handle it all. You can easily sort, filter, and analyze your data to gain valuable insights and make informed decisions.

Excel also offers a variety of formatting options to make your data visually appealing and easy to understand. You can apply different fonts, colors, and styles to your cells, as well as create conditional formatting rules to highlight important information. This makes it easier to present your data in a clear and professional manner.

Collaboration is another strength of Excel. With the ability to share workbooks and collaborate in real-time, multiple users can work together on a single spreadsheet, making it ideal for team projects or data analysis. You can track changes, leave comments, and ensure everyone is on the same page.

Excel is not limited to just numbers. You can also use it to manage lists, create calendars, and even build simple databases. Its versatility and flexibility make it a valuable tool for a wide range of tasks and projects.

In conclusion, Microsoft Excel is a powerful and versatile program that allows you to organize, analyze, and visualize data effectively. Whether you're a student, professional, or business owner, Excel can help streamline your work and improve productivity. With its extensive range of features and user-friendly interface, Excel is a must-have tool for anyone dealing with data. So, dive in, explore its capabilities, and unlock the full potential of Microsoft Excel.

Chapter 1: Overview of the Excel Objects and Interface

In the previous section, we were introduced to the capabilities of Excel. This section will focus on understanding the various tools within Excel that assist us in performing our tasks, along with an overview of the Excel interface.

1.1 Exploring the Excel Environment

Upon initiating a new Excel file, the Excel environment typically presents the following features:

1.1.1 Ribbon or Menu Bar

This section provides a variety of tools and options essential for working with Excel and carrying out our tasks effectively.

1.1.2 Address Bar

The Address Bar displays the object name, active range, or cell. You can enter the name of the object to activate it within this bar.

1.1.3 Formula Bar

The Formula Bar allows us to input and edit formulas within cells or objects in Excel.

1.1.4 Windows or Application Button

This button allows you to minimize, maximize, or exit the Excel application, providing essential control over the window interface.

1.1.5 Status Bar

The status bar displays the current status of tasks within the application. Additionally, it allows for printing the status using VBA (Visual Basic for Applications).

1.1.6 Zoom

The zoom feature enables users to adjust the magnification levels of the worksheets, allowing for increased or decreased visibility of the content.

1.1.7 Quick Access Tool Bar

Apart from the ribbon, which houses the majority of Excel commands, there is a small collection of commonly used commands situated on a special toolbar at the top of the window in Excel. This toolbar is designed for quick access to these frequently used commands. The Quick Access Toolbar allows users to assign frequently used tools for quick and easy access, enhancing efficiency when working with Excel.

1.2 Working with Excel Objects

In Excel, various objects like cells, ranges, worksheets, workbooks, rows, and columns are fundamental elements that you will frequently interact with. As we move forward, we will explore these objects in more detail to deepen your understanding of Excel functionality.

1.2.1 Excel Workbook

The workbook functions as the primary file that can be named and stored in a chosen folder. All other elements, such as worksheets and charts, are contained within this workbook as integral components.

1.2.2 Worksheet

A worksheet provides the space where you can input and format your data. Multiple worksheets come together to form a workbook, allowing for the organization and management of related information.

1.2.3 Cell
Cells are box-like elements within the worksheet used for entering data and formulas.

1.2.4 Range
A range refers to a grouping of cells within a worksheet in Excel.

1.2.5 Rows
Rows in Excel are horizontal collections of cells that are identified by numbers. They provide a structure for organizing and displaying data within a worksheet. Each row is represented by a number and extends from left to right across the spreadsheet.

1.2.6 Columns
Columns in Excel are vertical sets of cells identified by letters along the top of the worksheet. They provide a way to organize and manage data, allowing users to input and analyze information in a structured manner. Each column is represented by a letter and extends from top to bottom across the spreadsheet.

1.3 Excel Ribbon: A Quick Overview

Similar to other Office applications, the Excel ribbon serves as the main interface, housing all the features and commands essential for your tasks. To discover the full potential of Excel, simply delve into the ribbon and explore its capabilities.

The Microsoft Excel ribbon consists of tabs and icons located at the top of the Excel window, enabling users to easily locate, comprehend, and utilize commands for specific tasks. It resembles a somewhat intricate toolbar, serving the purpose of one.

Initially introduced in Excel 2007, the ribbon replaced the traditional toolbars and pull-down menus featured in earlier versions. Furthermore, with the release of Excel 2010, Microsoft incorporated the option to customize the ribbon, offering users a tailored experience.

The Excel ribbon comprises four fundamental elements: command buttons, dialog launchers, groups, and tabs.

Ribbon Tab: The ribbon tab comprises various commands logically categorized into groups.

Ribbon Group: A ribbon group consists of a collection of closely associated commands typically executed as part of a broader task.

Dialog Launcher: The dialog launcher is a little arrow located in the bottom-right corner of a group, which reveals additional related commands. These launchers are found in groups that encompass more commands than the available space permits.

Command Button: The command button is what you click to execute a specific action.

1.3.1 Introduction to the Ribbon Tab

The ribbon in Excel includes the following tabs, arranged from left to right:

1.3.1.1 File Tab

This tab provides access to the backstage view, where you can access important file-related Excel options and commands. It was added in Excel 2010 to replace the Office button in Excel 2007 and the File menu in previous versions.

1.3.1.2 Home Tab

This section houses commonly used commands such as formatting, filtering, sorting, pasting, and copying.

1.3.1.3 Insert Tab

This tab is used to add various objects to a worksheet, including footers, headers, equations, special symbols, hyperlinks, pivot tables, charts, and images.

1.3.1.4 Draw Tab

Depending on the type of device, you can draw using a finger, mouse, or digital pen. This tab is accessible in Excel 2013 and later versions, but it's not visible by default, similar to the Developer tab.

1.3.1.5 Page Layout Tab

This section offers tools to manage the appearance of the worksheet, both on the screen and when printed. These tools allow you to control the print area, align objects, set page margins, adjust gridlines, and manage theme settings.

1.3.1.6 Formulas Tab

This section comprises tools for adding functions, creating names, and managing calculation settings.

1.3.1.7 Data Tab

This section contains the tools for managing the data within the worksheet and establishing connections to external data sources.

1.3.1.8 Review Tab

This section enables you to protect workbooks and worksheets, insert notes and comments, track changes, and check your spelling.

1.3.1.9 View Tab

This section offers commands for managing multiple windows, freezing panes, and switching between worksheet views.

1.3.1.10 Help Tab

This tab is available in Office 365 and Excel 2019. It gives you quick access to the Help Task Pane, training videos, feature suggestions, feedback submission, and contact with Microsoft support.

1.3.1.11 Developer Tab

Developer: This section grants access to sophisticated features like XML commands, ActiveX and Form controls, and VBA macros. It's initially hidden and requires enabling.

1.3.1.12 Add-ins Tab

This feature is visible only when you launch an older workbook or load an add-in that personalizes the menu or toolbars.

1.3.2 Contextual Ribbon Tabs

In Excel, apart from the regular tabs, there are contextual tabs known as tool tabs. These tabs appear only when you select specific items, such as a picture, shape, chart, or table. For instance, if you choose a chart, the Design and Format tabs will become visible under Chart Tools.

1.3.3 Minimizing or Hiding the Excel Ribbon

If you want to maximize the space for your worksheet data, particularly when using a computer that has a small screen, you can minimize the ribbon by pressing the Ctrl + F1 shortcut.

You also have the option to fully hide the ribbon when you click on the Ribbon Display Options button located at the top-right corner of the Excel window and then select Auto-hide Ribbon. This allows you to free up more space on the interface, providing a more focused view of your worksheet.

1.3.4 Restoring Missing Commands and Unhiding the Excel Ribbon

If you find that every command has vanished from your ribbon and only the tab names can be seen, simply press Ctrl + F1 to restore them all to their normal state.

In the event that you can't find the whole thing, click the Ribbon Display Options button and select Show Tabs and Commands to bring it back into view.

1.3.5 Customizing the Excel Ribbon

If you want to tailor the ribbon to suit your specific needs and have quick access to the tools you use most, you can easily customize it.

To access the customization options, simply right-click on the ribbon and choose "Customize the Ribbon" from the context menu. This will open the Customize Ribbon window under Excel Options, allowing you to personalize the ribbon according to your preferences.

Once in the Customize Ribbon window, you have the freedom to add your own tabs containing your preferred commands, rename, hide, or show tabs, reorder groups and tabs, and perform various other customization options to tailor the ribbon to your specific requirements.

1.3.6 Displaying the Developer Tab and Other Hidden Tabs on the Ribbon

The Developer tab is a valuable addition to the Excel ribbon, providing access to a range of futuristic features like XML commands, ActiveX and Form controls, VBA macros, and more. However, it is initially hidden. Fortunately, enabling it is a straightforward process.

- Simply right-click the ribbon.
- Choose "Customize the Ribbon."
- Under Main Tabs, select "Developer."
- Hit the OK button.

Similarly, it is possible to display other tabs, such as the Draw tab, that are available in Excel but not initially visible on the ribbon using the same method.

1.4 Introduction to the Formula Bar

1.4.1 Defining the Formula Bar

The Formula Bar is the area where formulas or data entered into a worksheet for the active cell are displayed. It also serves as a tool for editing the formula or data within the active cell.

While the active cell shows the results of its formula, the actual formula can be viewed and edited in the Formula Bar.

1.4.2 Adjusting the Size of the Formula Bar

You have the option to expand the formula bar either horizontally or vertically based on your specific requirements.

- Expanding the formula bar horizontally is straightforward. If you wish to do this, simply position the mouse cursor between the Formula Bar and the Name Box until it changes into a horizontal double-ended arrow. Then, click and drag to make changes to the horizontal size as per your preference.
- For vertical expansion of the Formula Bar, move your cursor to the lowest part of the Formula Bar area until the cursor transforms into a vertical double-ended arrow. Then, left-click and drag to make changes to the vertical size according to your preference.
- You can quickly adjust the Formula Bar by using the expand or contract toggle located on the right-hand side of the Formula Bar. Simply use this toggle to expand or contract the formula bar as needed.
- To hide the Formula Bar completely, navigate to the View tab and deselect the Formula Bar option.

1.4.3 Using the Formula Bar to Enter and Edit Data

To enter data into any cell, follow these steps:

- Begin by selecting the cell where you would like to enter your data and starting to type.
- While typing the data, observe that it also shows up in the formula bar.
- You can either press Enter on your keyboard or click the check mark to accept the data. To get rid of the data, simply press Esc or click the X button.

When entering a formula, remember that every formula should begin with "=" (only the equals sign without the quotation marks). To edit any formula or data in a cell, simply choose the cell and press F2 to enter editing mode, or click into the Formula Bar.

1.5 Understanding Excel's Fundamental Operations

1.5.1 The Basics of Data Entry in Excel

Microsoft Excel is a valuable tool for arranging, studying, and preserving data. Its grid-based layout consists of cells, rows, and columns, serving as the foundation for any spreadsheet. Proficiency in navigating and entering data into these elements is essential for utilizing Excel efficiently.

1.5.2 Defining a Cell

A cell is where a row and a column meet, acting as the fundamental unit for inputting and storing data in a spreadsheet.

Every cell has a unique address, formed by combining the column letter and row number. For instance, the cell in the third column and the third row is referred to as cell C3.

1.5.2.1 How to Enter Data in Cells

To input data into cells:

- Select a cell by clicking on it. The selected cell will be outlined by a border.
- Begin to type to input data. Hit the Enter key on your keyboard to proceed to the next row, or the Tab button to proceed to the next column.
- To edit the data entered in a cell, select it, double-click on it, and start typing to modify the existing data, or use the F2 button on your keyboard to directly edit the cell.

1.5.3 Defining a Row

In Excel, a row is a horizontal line of cells identified by a number on the left side of the spreadsheet. It provides a way to organize and categorize data across the spreadsheet.

1.5.3.1 How to Enter Data into Rows

- Click on the row number to choose the entire row.
- To enter data in sequence, select the initial cell in the row, start typing, and then utilize the Tab key on your keyboard to proceed to the following cell in the same row.

1.5.4 Defining a Column?

In Excel, a column refers to a vertical series of cells identified by letters at the top of the spreadsheet, such as A, B, C, and so on. Columns are great for organizing data into categories like financial figures, dates, or names.

1.5.4.1 How to Enter Data into a Column

- Click on the column letter to choose the whole column.
- Select the top cell and enter your data to input data in a column, and use the Enter key on your keyboard to proceed to the next row within the same column.

1.6 Simple Formatting Methods

Here, we explore the formatting methods essential for creating neat and refined presentations of your work.

1.6.1 Number Formatting

While number formats may seem straightforward, using them incorrectly can result in inaccurate reports.

Let's consider this example:. Imagine you work at a clothing store, and your manager asks you to identify the customer who made the highest purchase in the month to offer them a discount on their next purchase.

Suppose every transaction is recorded in dollars except for one. In a rush, you forgot to add the dollar format to this transaction, which also happens to be the biggest one for the month. This example demonstrates how things can easily become complicated.

In this section, you will discover what number formatting entails in Excel and how to apply it effectively.

Number formatting in Excel can be achieved through the following simple steps:

- To apply number formatting, choose a cell, a range of cells, or the entire column where you want to add the formatting.
- Proceed to the Home button and click on it.
- Click on the dropdown in the Number Group to access the number formatting.

There's a simpler alternative method available:

- Choose a cell, a cell range, or a whole column.
- Perform a right-click on any selected cell. A drop-down menu will show up. Choose "Format cells" from the menu.

1.6.2 Cell Formatting

Formatting cells in Excel involves adjusting text alignment, images, cell background color, font, and text color, which differs from number formatting in Excel.

To begin, let's explore the font choices available in cell formatting within Excel:

- Go to the Home tab and locate the Font group.
- Select the drop-down symbol to access a diverse range of font options offered by Excel.

Following the Font option, you can explore the underline, italic, and bold choices, font color, and text alignment within the Home tab. Slightly to the right in the alignment group, you'll find text indentation, text wrapping, and text alignment options.

1.7 Simple Mathematical Operations

You can use six main arithmetic operators for calculations in Excel:

- Addition (+)
- Subtraction (-)
- Multiplication (*)
- Division (/)
- Percent (%)
- Exponentiation (^)

Just as their names indicate, each of these operators is capable of carrying out a specific calculation. This section will guide us on using these operators effectively.

When working with these operators in Excel, you'll need to initiate the formula with (=) to perform any calculation. To input these operators, simply use the corresponding keys on your keyboard.

1.7.1 Addition (+)

The addition operator allows you to find the sum of two or more values.

Example:

$=value1 + value2$

$=200 + 300$

In the above example, we used the addition operator (+) to calculate the sum of 200 and 300. You can also make use of cell references in the same manner.

1.7.2 Subtraction (-)

The subtraction operator gives you the opportunity to subtract one value from another. Similar to the previous example, you can either use direct input values or cell references.

1.7.3 Multiplication (*)

To multiply values in Excel, utilize the asterisk operator, which can be inserted using the corresponding key on your keyboard. Similarly, you can directly input the values within the formula. For example:

=500*30

1.7.4 Division (/)

To perform division in Excel, use the forward slash (/) as the division operator. For instance:

=Dividend/Divisor

You can also directly enter the values into the formula.

1.7.5 Percent (%)

You can use the percentage operator to change a number value to a percentage. Simply make use of the percentage key on your keyboard to enter the percentage operator after entering a number in the cell. If you would like to find the percentage of a value, you can utilize the multiply (asterisk) operator to do that.

1.7.6 Exponent (^)

You can make use of the exponent operator to raise a number to a power. For instance, you can directly enter the exponent operator and specify the number to raise to the desired power. This functionality can be used to calculate the cube, square, square root, and more.

Chapter 2: Formulas and Functions

A function in an Excel spreadsheet is a preset formula designed to carry out calculations using certain values in a special sequence. Excel typically offers common functions for swiftly determining the minimum value, maximum value, count, average, and sum for a cell range. To utilize functions effectively, it's important to grasp the various components of a function, especially how to construct arguments to calculate cell references and values.

2.1 The Difference Between Formulas and Functions

2.1.1 Formulas

A formula is an expression that performs operations on values in a single cell or within a cell range in Excel. For

instance, the formula =B1+B2+B3 calculates the sum of
the values in the range from cell B1 to B3.

2.1.2 Functions

In Excel, functions are preset formulas that simplify the
arduous manual typing of formulas by providing them with
user-friendly names. For instance, the function
=SUM(B1:B3) sums every value from B1 to B3.

2.2 Parts of a Function

For a function to work properly, it must adhere to a certain
format, known as syntax. The fundamental syntax for any
function in Excel consists of an equals sign (=), the
function name (such as SUM), and a number of arguments.
Arguments hold the data you would like to calculate.

2.2.1 Understanding Arguments

Arguments in functions can make reference to both a single
cell and a cell range, and they need to be enclosed in
parentheses. The number of arguments you include
depends on the specific syntax needed for the function.

For instance, the function =AVERAGE(C1:C9) calculates
the average of the values within the cell range C1:C9,
demonstrating the use of a single argument in the function.

When using multiple arguments in a function, they need to be separated by a comma. For instance, the function =SUM(B1:B3, D1:D2, F2) adds the values of every cell within the three specified arguments.

2.3 Absolute and Relative References

In Excel, each cell has a unique reference indicating its location within the spreadsheet.

These references are utilized in formulas to perform calculations, and the fill function can be employed to extend formulas horizontally, upwards, and even downwards.

Excel comprises two types of cell references:

- Absolute references
- Relative reference

When working in Excel, an absolute cell reference is a directive that instructs Excel to lock a cell reference in place.

To make a reference absolute, the dollar sign ($) is utilized.

- Relative reference example: D5
- Absolute reference example: D5

2.3.1 Absolute Cell Reference

An absolute reference is denoted by the presence of a dollar sign ($). This effectively locks the reference into the formula.

To utilize absolute references, simply add a dollar sign ($) to the formula.

2.3.1.1 Understanding the Dollar Sign in Absolute Cell Reference

The dollar sign in Excel can have three independent states:

- Absolute for both row and column, where the reference is completely locked. For instance: =D5
- Absolute for the column, which locks the cell reference to the column while the row continues to be relative. For instance: =$D5

- Absolute for the row, which locks the cell reference to the row while the column keeps being relative. For instance: =D$5

2.3.2 Relative Cell Reference

By default, cell references in Excel are relative and do not have a dollar sign ($).

Relative references free the cells from specific references, allowing the fill function to carry on with the order without constraints.

2.4 Simple Excel Functions

Now that you know how to insert functions and formulas appropriately, let us explore some basic Excel functions to help you get started.

2.4.1 SUM

The SUM function is a fundamental formula in the Excel program. It typically adds values from a chosen range of rows or columns.

It is used as follows:

=SUM(number1, [number2], …)

Examples:

- =SUM(C2:H2): Adds up the values in the row C2 to H2.
- =SUM(B2:B8): Adds up the values in the column B2 to B8.
- =SUM(D2:D7, D9, D12:D15): Adds values from the cell range D2 to D7, jumps D8, sums D9, skips D10 and D11, then lastly sums from D12 to D15.
- =SUM(B2:B8)/20: Demonstrates turning the function into a formula.

2.4.2 AVERAGE

The AVERAGE function calculates an average of given data, such as calculating the average delivery time for a series of shipments or finding the average time spent on different tasks over a period.

It is used as follows:

=AVERAGE(number1, [number2], …)

Example:

=AVERAGE(A2:A11) – Demonstrates a straightforward average, which is also much the same as using (SUM(A2:A11)/10).

2.4.3 COUNT

The COUNT function is used to count every cell in a specified range that contains only number values.

It is used as follows:

=COUNT(value1, [value2], …)

Examples:

- COUNT(D:D): This example will count every number value in column D. Be that as it may, you will have to make changes to the range within the formula to count rows.

- COUNT(D1:F1): It now has the ability to count rows.

2.4.4 COUNTA

The COUNTA function is used to count every cell in a specified range, just like the COUNT function. In spite of that, it will count every cell without considering its type. Unlike COUNT, which can only count numbers, the COUNTA function also counts text, empty strings, errors, logical values, strings, times, or dates.

It is used as follows:

=COUNTA(value1, [value2], …)

Example:

COUNTA(A3:A14): Counts rows 3 to 14 in "column A" without consideration of their type. However, similar to COUNT, you cannot count rows using the same formula. You would need to change the selection within the parenthesis; for instance, COUNTA(D2:J2) will count columns D to J.

2.4.5 IF

The IF function is commonly used to organize data based on specific criteria. One of its advantages is the ability to include other functions and formulas within it.

It is structured as follows:

=IF(logical_test, [value_if_true], [value_if_false])

Example usage:

- =IF(A3<B3,"TRUE","FALSE"): This expression is used to check if the value in A3 is less than the value in B3. If true, it assigns the value of the cell as true; if not, it's false.
- =IF(SUM(B1:B10) > SUM(C1:C10), SUM(B1:B10), SUM(C1:C10)) – This demonstrates a more advanced IF statement. Before anything else, it will sum B1:B10 and C1:C10, then compare the totals. If the total of B1:B10 is greater than the total of C1:C10, it assigns the cell value as the total of B1:B10.

2.4.6 TRIM

The TRIM function is used to eliminate extra spaces in your data, preventing errors in your functions. It works on a single cell and removes all empty spaces.

Usage:

=TRIM(text)

Example:

TRIM (G2): This gets rid of possible empty spaces in the value in cell G2.

2.4.7 MIN and MAX

The MIN and MAX functions are useful for identifying the smallest and largest numbers within a set of values.

To use the MIN function, you can write:

=MIN(number1, [number2], …)

For instance:

=MIN(C2:D11): This will find the smallest number between column C from C2 and column D from D2 to row 11 in both columns C and D.

Similarly, for the MAX function, the syntax is:

=*MAX(number1, [number2], …)*

For instance:

=MAX(C2:D11): This identifies the largest number between column C from C2 and column D from D2 to row 11 in both columns C and D.

2.5 An Introduction to Logical Functions

The logical function feature enables us to make decisions while executing functions and formulas. Logical functions are utilized to:

- Ascertain whether a given condition is true or not.
- Put together multiple conditions at once.

2.5.1 How Important is a Condition, and What Does It Mean?

A condition is a statement that can be either true or false. This statement could be a function that checks if the value entered in a cell is text or numeric, if a value is less than, equal to, or greater than a given value, and so on.

Let's consider an example using the IF function:

In this section, we'll focus on home supplies. Suppose we have a list of home supplies in Column A and their respective budget amounts in Column B. We can utilize the IF function to categorize supplies as overpriced or not. For instance, we can surmise that supplies with a value greater than 5,000 are costly, while those less than 5,000 are considered less expensive.

To achieve this, you can use the following formula with the IF function:

=IF(B11<5000,"Yes","No")

Here's a breakdown of the formula:

. "=IF(...)" invokes the IF function.

. "B11<5000" represents the condition that the IF function assesses, checking if the subtotal value of cell B11 is lesser than 5,000.

. "Yes" is the value displayed if the B11 value is lesser than 5,000.

. "No" is the value displayed if the B11 value is more than 5,000.

. After inputting the formula, press the enter key to obtain the desired results.

2.5.2 An Explanation of Excel's Logic Functions
Here are a few of the logical functions available in Excel:

2.5.3 AND Function
This function is used to check more than one condition, and it will return true only if every condition is true.

For instance, using the formula =AND(5 > 0, ISNUMBER(5)) will result in TRUE because both conditions are true.

2.5.4 IF Function

This function checks if a condition is satisfied. It returns true if the condition is satisfied. It returns false if the condition is not satisfied.

Usage: For instance, using the formula =IF(ISNUMBER(15), "Yes", "No") will return "Yes" because 15 is a number, thus meeting the condition.

2.5.5 FALSE Function

The logical value of false will be returned by this function. It is employed in the comparison of the results of a function or condition that will either return true or false.

To use it, you will write: FALSE()

2.5.6 NOT Function

This function returns false if the condition is true and true if the condition is not.

For example, using the formula =NOT(ISNUMBER(A)) will return true. This happens because ISNUMBER(A) will return false, and the NOT function will convert false to true.

2.5.7 IFNA Function

A function or formula that returns a #N/A error indicates that a value is not available. The IFNA function will return a specified NA value if there is an #N/A error. It will also return a specified value if the error doesn't occur.

For example, using the formula =IFNA(A7*D7, 0) will return 0 if either A7 or D7 is empty, indicating the absence of a value.

2.5.8 TRUE Function

When in use, this function will return the logical value TRUE. It compares the output of a function or condition that returns true or false.

To use it, you will write: TRUE()

2.5.9 OR Function

This function is used when the conditions you intend to evaluate are more than one. It will return true if all or any of the conditions are true, and false if all of the conditions are false.

For example, using the formula =OR(A6="trade", B6="sales") will return true if either or both A6 and B6 contain "trade" or "sales."

2.6 Error Handling in Formulas

The IFERROR function is the go-to function used to capture and handle errors in any formula. IFERROR outputs a defined value if the formula evaluates to an error; if there are no errors, it returns the actual outcome of the formula.

It is structured like this:

IFERROR(value, value_if_error)

It has the following arguments:

value: This is required. It is the argument that is examined for an error.

value_if_error: This is also required. It is the value that the formula returns if it evaluates to an error. The function evaluates error types, such as

#NULL!, #NAME?, #NUM!, #DIV/0!, #REF!, #VALUE!, or #N/A.

Notes

- If any of the two arguments above is an empty cell, the IFERROR function will consider it an empty-string value ("").
- When the value is an array formula, the IFERROR function outputs an array of results for every cell in the defined range of value.

Chapter 3: Data Management

3.1 Overview of Excel's Sort and Filter Features

Excel, a widely used spreadsheet program, goes beyond simple text and number input. It's a robust tool for arranging and examining data. Whether you're a beginner or need a quick refresher, this section provides a thorough overview of Excel's sort and filter features. We'll delve into the fundamentals, explain the syntax, and present practical examples to make managing your data easier.

3.2 Learning to Work with Excel Data

Before we get into sorting and filtering, it's important to comprehend the type of data we'll be dealing with. In Excel, you have the ability to generate spreadsheets with columns and rows, each housing distinct information. This data can include various types, such as text, numbers, dates, and more complex data formats.

3.3 Data Sorting in Excel

Next, we'll cover how to sort data by a single column and also by multiple columns. Let's get started:

3.3.1 Data Sorting Using Just One Column

When it comes to sorting your data in Excel, you can easily sort it by a single column. Let's walk through the simple steps:

- Select your preferred column: Start by clicking on the header of the column you want to sort.
- Navigate to the "Data" tab. Once you've selected the column, head over to the "Data" tab in Excel.
- Choose the Sorting Order: If you want your data sorted in ascending order, click on "Sort A to Z;" otherwise, "Sort Z to A" for descending order.

Suppose you have a list of names in column A, specifically from A1 to A10, and you're looking to arrange them alphabetically. You can follow the steps for sorting data by a single column above to sort the list of names in ascending order.

3.3.2 Data Sorting Using Several Columns

When it comes to precisely organizing your data in Excel, sorting by multiple columns can be incredibly useful. Here's a simple method to achieve this:

- Choose the Data Range: Start by selecting the range of data that you want to sort based on multiple columns.
- Navigate to the "Data" tab.
- Initiate Sorting: Click on "Sort" to begin the sorting process.
- Identify Sorting Criteria: Specify the columns you would like to sort by and the sorting order for each column.

So, if you've got a list with names in column D and ages in column E, and you would like to tidy it up by name in ascending order and then by age in descending order, here's what you do: Begin by sorting the whole data by names in ascending order, and then sort the outcome by age in descending order.

3.4 Excel Data Filtering

Let's see how to filter through data based on a single criterion.

3.4.1 Filtering Data Using a Single Criteria

When you filter your data, it allows you to show just the rows that fit certain conditions. Let's dive into the process:

- First, pick the range you wish to filter.
- Navigate to the "Data" tab.
- Locate and click on the "Filter" option.
- Pick out the criteria you'd like to use for filtering in the filter dropdown for a specific column.

Consider this scenario: you have a list of items in column C paired with their respective prices in column D. To filter through and isolate items with prices greater than $100, follow these steps:

- Highlight the data range (C1:D10).
- Head over to the "Data" tab.
- Opt for the "Filter" option.
- Within the filter dropdown for column D, navigate to "Number Filters," then select "Greater Than," and input 100.

3.5 Sorting and Filtering Tricks and Tips

You can improve the efficiency of sorting and filtering your data with these helpful tips and tricks:

- Speed up data sorting and filtering by making use of keyboard shortcuts.
- Elevate your data analysis game by combining sorting and filtering for more advanced insights.
- Ensure data consistency by applying data validation techniques.

3.6 A Brief Overview of Conditional Formatting

Conditional formatting in Excel lets you customize the appearance of cells based on specific criteria. This feature aids in interpreting data and identifying notable trends.

3.6.1 Using Conditional Formatting to Highlight Cells

Let's begin by highlighting cells with values exceeding 400. Follow these steps:

- Choose the cell range you would like to highlight.
- Navigate to the Home tab, locate the Styles Group, and select Conditional Formatting.
- Opt for Highlight Cell Rules, then select Greater Than.

- Input your preferred value and choose the formatting style.
- Click OK to apply the changes.

3.6.2 How to Clear Formatting

To get rid of any applied formatting rules, take the following steps:

- Choose the cell range with the applied formatting.
- Navigate to the Home tab, find the Styles Group, and select Conditional Formatting.
- Select Clear Rules, then Clear Rules from Selected Cells.

3.7 Managing Vast Datasets and Cutting Out Duplicate Data

When dealing with vast amounts of data in Excel, there's a chance you might encounter duplicates. This segment will guide you in identifying and removing them.

3.7.1 Finding Duplicates in Your Spreadsheet

If your goal is to identify duplicates for potential deletion without actually removing them, the most effective method is to highlight all duplicate content using conditional formatting.

- Firstly, choose the data you would like to examine for duplicate information. Next, head to the Home tab, and under Conditional Formatting, select Highlight Cell Rules, and then click on Duplicate Values.

- In the Conditional Formatting window, proceed to the "Format with" drop-down menu to choose the color scheme for highlighting duplicates. Once selected, click Done. For better readability, consider opting for a high-contrast color scheme like light red fill.

- Now, take a moment to examine the duplicate data and determine if there's any unwanted information you'd like to remove.

3.7.2 How to Get Rid of Redundant Data in Excel

If your aim is to locate and remove duplicates in Excel without the need for manual review, there are two straightforward methods to achieve this.

- Begin by clicking on any cell containing data. Afterward, go to the Data tab and select Remove Duplicates.

- In the Remove Duplicates window, choose the columns you want to consider for finding unwanted data. Hit the OK button. (Remember, the Remove

Duplicates tool permanently erases any duplicate data, so consider copying the original data to a different worksheet for future use.)

- Excel will provide information on the number of duplicates successfully removed.

3.8 Working with Excel's Data Validation

Excel's Data Validation serves to limit (validate) user input within a worksheet. In essence, it involves establishing a validation rule that governs the type of data permissible in a particular cell.

Let's explore a variety of functions that Excel's data validation brings to the table:

- Permits only text or numbers in a cell.
- Enable data entries of a particular length.
- Limit to numbers within a set range.
- Constrain entries to a choice from a drop-down list.
- Confine times and dates to a specified range.
- Display a custom message when a user chooses a cell.
- Validate an entry based on information from another cell.
- Identify errors in validated cells.

- Display a warning message for incorrectly entered data.

Consider this scenario: you establish a rule that confines data input to 5-digit numbers ranging from 10000 to 99999. If a user enters something different, Excel promptly presents an error alert, clarifying the mistake made.

3.8.1 How to Use Excel for Data Validation

To implement data validation in Excel, follow these simple steps:

1. To initiate the process of data validation, choose the cells you would like to validate. Proceed to the Data tab, find the Data Tools group, and select the button for Data Validation.

Alternatively, you can press the Alt, D and L keys on your keyboard to access the dialog box labeled "Data Validation," pressing the keys one at a time.

2. Establish an Excel validation rule based on your specific requirements on the Settings tab. For the criteria, you have the flexibility to input any option in the following:

Values: You can enter numbers directly into the criteria boxes.

Cell references: You can also establish a rule that depends on a formula or value from another cell.

Formulas: Lastly, you can enable the expression of more elaborate conditions.

Once you've set up the validation rule, you can switch to a separate tab to include an error warning or an input message, or you can hit the OK button to exit the Data Validation window.

3. If you wish to provide users with a message explaining the allowed data in a specific cell, follow these steps on the Input Message tab:

a) Enable the "Show input message when cell is selected" box by clicking to check it.

b) Input the text and title of your message into the respective fields.

c) Hit the OK button to exit the dialog window.

Once the user chooses the cell to which you applied validation, the input message you added will promptly appear.

4. Optionally, alongside the input message, you have the option to display one of the subsequent error alerts when an invalid entry is made in a cell.

a) Stop (this is the default alert type).

It is the most stringent alert type, preventing users from inputting invalid data. Select the Retry button to input another value or Cancel to clear the entry.

b) Warning

This alert type notifies users about invalid data without prohibiting entry. Select the Yes option to input the invalid entry, No to modify it, or Cancel to clear the entry.

c) Information

This is the most lenient type of alert, merely informing users when they enter data that is invalid. Hit the OK button to input the invalid value, or cancel to clear it from the cell.

3.8.2 Setting Up a Personalized Error Message

To set up a personalized error message, navigate to the Error Alert tab and specify the following details:

- Ensure the "Show error alert after invalid data is entered" box is checked (usually preselected).
- Choose the preferred alert type from the Style box.
- Input the text and title of the error message into the respective boxes.
- Hit the OK option to confirm.

Now, when a user inputs data that is invalid, Excel will showcase a distinctive alert detailing the error.

Please keep in mind that if you don't add your custom message, the preselected Stop alert will appear with generic text.

3.9 Simple Text Functions

Text functions play a pivotal role in enhancing productivity and minimizing the time invested in managing substantial amounts of text-oriented data in the Excel spreadsheet. Below, you'll find various types of text functions in Excel, along with examples.

3.9.1 LEFT Function

This function retrieves a specified number of characters from the left side of a text. For instance, if you wish to retrieve six characters from the left of the text in cell A3, use the following formula:

=LEFT(A3, 6)

3.9.2 MID Function

This function in the Excel spreadsheet is designed to pull characters from the middle of a string. To illustrate, if you would like to pull five characters from the middle of the text in C6, commencing from the eighth character, the syntax is:

=MID(C6, 8, 5)

It's essential to note that spaces are counted as characters in the MID function.

3.9.3 RIGHT Function

Much like the left function, you can use this function to retrieve characters from the right side of the text. For instance, to retrieve eight characters from the right side of your text in cell D5, you would use the following syntax:

=RIGHT(D5, 8)

3.9.4 FIND Function

The FIND function in Excel indicates the position of the first character of a specified phrase within a text. For example, to locate the position of the letters "or" in the word "Hardwork" in cell E8, you would use the following syntax:

=FIND("or", E8)

It's worth noting that the FIND function in Excel works like the SEARCH function, with the key distinction being that FIND is case-sensitive, whereas SEARCH isn't.

3.9.5 LEN Function
In Excel, the LEN function serves to determine the length of characters within a designated cell. The usage is as follows:

=LEN(A2)

3.9.6 REPT Function
In Excel, the REPT function duplicates a specified text multiple times. For instance, if you want to replicate the phrase "Merry Christmas" in cell E8 seven times, you can use the following formula:

=REPT(E8,7)

This formula reproduces the text without introducing spaces.

3.9.7 PROPER Function

In Excel, the PROPER function capitalizes the initial letter of every word in a designated cell. The syntax for the illustrated example is:

=PROPER(E8)

3.9.8 UPPER Function

This function in Excel transforms every lowercase text within a specified cell into uppercase text. The formula for this is:

=UPPER(E8)

3.9.9 TRIM Function

The TRIM function in Excel is designed to eliminate additional spaces preceding the text or between words within a cell. The formula for the provided example is:

=TRIM(E8)

3.9.10 SUBSTITUTE Function

The SUBSTITUTE function in Excel is handy for replacing specific text within a string with new content. To implement this, you must enclose both the existing and new text in double inverted commas ("[example]"). In the following example, if we would like to remove the word Genius put back the word Genuine in cell E8, the substitution formula would be:

=SUBSTITUTE(E8,"Genius","Genuine")

It's crucial to note that the SUBSTITUTE function is case-sensitive. It won't execute the replacement if the case of the old text doesn't precisely match that of the provided text.

3.9.11 LOWER Function

This function in Excel changes text from uppercase to lowercase. It functions as the reverse of the UPPER function. The formula for the provided example is:

=LOWER(E8)

3.9.12 CONCATENATE Function

The CONCATENATE function in Excel is a handy tool for combining text from multiple cells. If, for instance, you wish to merge the text from cells D3, E3, and F3, you can use the following syntax:

=CONCATENATE(D3, E3, F3)

This formula seamlessly brings together the text from all of these cells into a single cell without introducing any spaces.

To include spaces between the text from different cells, a simple approach is to insert " " (a space within double quotation marks) between every cell value. For instance, to incorporate spaces in the above example, the formula would be:

=CONCATENATE(D3, " ", E3, " ", F3)

Chapter 4: Data Visualization

Creating graphs and charts stands out as one of the most effective methods for presenting data in a manner that is both clear and easily understood.

4.1 What Exactly Is an Excel Graph or Chart?

A chart or graph in Excel serves as a visual depiction of the data within an Excel spreadsheet. These visual representations enable users to extract insights, recognize patterns, make comparisons, and identify trends from the data. Excel offers a variety of alternatives for charts and graphs, ranging from pie charts to line graphs and bar graphs.

If you're dealing with data in Excel and looking to present it visually, charts or graphs can be helpful tools. For large datasets, converting the data into a graph can simplify comprehension, eliminating the need to pore over every single number. However, for smaller datasets that are easily understandable at a glance, creating graphs may not be necessary.

If you want to delve deeper into your data than just the numbers, like comparing different sets or tracking changes over time, using a graph or chart is a wise choice.

Here are some practical ways you can use charts and graphs:

- Use a pie chart to display percentage ratios and proportions.
- Track changes over time using a line graph.
- Compare values using bar and column graphs.

4.2 Graph or Chart Types in Excel

In MS Excel, the possibilities extend beyond the typical line or bar charts. Recognizing the distinct purposes of every chart type empowers you to extract more meaningful insights for your projects or team. Here are some excellent choices at your disposal:

4.2.1 Bar Graph

In Excel, a bar graph is a visual representation of data arranged horizontally. This format facilitates the comparison of various data sets and the observation of trends over a period of time. It's also effective for showcasing proportions between different data elements or categories.

For practical applications, a bar graph can be employed to assess the sales performance of several products over months or quarters. This insight helps in determining which products to prioritize during specific time frames.

4.2.2 Area Chart

Excel's area charts serve as a valuable tool to observe trends, whether they're another variable or over time. Functioning much like a line graph, area charts add a visual dimension by coloring in sections, highlighting progression, and providing a feeling of volume.

Additionally, the stacked area chart option proves useful for comparing variations and trends across unrelated variables within several categories.

4.2.3 Line Graph

An efficient tool for observing trends over a period of time is the line graph, which offers simplicity without the additional elements of columns or bars. It enables the comparison of more than one data series effortlessly, like comparing organic visits from website A to website B over a 1-year period.

The line graph is effective in revealing the rate of change within a dataset. A sharp incline signifies a sudden surge in organic traffic. Conversely, a moderate decline indicates a slow decrease in traffic. Line graphs are particularly adept at identifying seasonal trends, such as drops or spikes linked to weather patterns or holidays.

4.2.4 Column Chart

A column chart in Excel resembles a bar graph, but it's oriented vertically instead of horizontally. It enables you to set various data elements in order based on their values. For example, if you wish to arrange sales figures across different states, a column chart can visually represent which states are performing better and which are lagging behind.

Similar to a bar graph, a column chart serves multiple purposes, including data comparison, trend visualization, and proportion analysis.

4.2.5 Spider (Radar) Chart

You may recognize a spider chart from personality tests, but its utility extends beyond that context. Spider charts present data within a multi-pointed, closed shape, typically incorporating several data points and variables. The size of this shape reflects the overall "value" of every included variable.

This chart type is ideal for comparing various data elements, including weaknesses, strengths, individual traits, entities, or attributes. Additionally, it aids in visualizing the distribution of data and identifying any significant skewness in the data set.

4.2.6 Pie Chart

A pie chart offers a convenient method of illustrating the proportional comparison between various data elements. Whether you're examining the percentage of natural traffic originating from website A vs. website B or evaluating market share relative to competitors, a pie chart provides a clear visualization of such data.

Moreover, it serves as a valuable tool for tracking advancement toward certain objectives. For example, if you would like to sell an item each day for thirty consecutive days, you can generate a pie chart to visualize the number of days you've achieved sales against the total target of 30.

4.2.7 Scatter Plot

A scatter plot resembles a line graph but serves a distinct purpose: it examines the connection between two variables, each represented on the X- and Y-axes. This allows you to discern patterns and correlations. For example, you could analyze the relationship between the natural traffic and the volume of sign-ups or leads.

If you notice a rise in trends, it indicates that your strategies to boost natural traffic are working. You can delve deeper by comparing the volume of signups and leads with daily conversions or sales.

Additional Excel chart options comprise stock charts, which track fluctuations in stock prices, and surface charts, which present data in a 3-dimensional layout.

4.3 Creating an Excel Graph or Chart

- Open Excel and input your data.
- Select from any of the nine available chart and graph options, such as a line graph.

- Select the cells containing your data, and proceed to the Insert tab.
- Navigate to the charts section and select the column icon. Then, pick your desired graph from the drop-down menu.

4.3.1 Switching What Is Shown on the X and Y Axis

To change the data displayed on the X and Y axes, follow these steps:

- Locate the bar graph and right-click on it.
- Choose "Select Data."
- Find and select "Switch Row/Column."

4.3.2 Modifying the Data's Colors and Layout (Legend, Axis Titles, and Chart Title)

Modify the arrangement and color of your data by following these steps.

- Locate the bar graph and click on it.
- Navigate to the Chart Design tab and click it. Here, you are allowed to select your preferred layout for the legend, axis titles, and chart title.

- For additional formatting of the legend, you can access the Format Legend Entry sidebar by clicking on the legend, which allows you to alter the fill color, affecting the color of the bars. To adjust other aspects of your chart, click on each element one by one, revealing the relative format window.

4.3.3 Axis and Legend Label Size Changes for Your Chart

Adjusting the size of your axis and legend labels is a simple task. After initially creating a chart or graph in Excel, you might find the labels to be small, based on the selected chart or graph type (line, pie, bar, etc.). To enhance readability, follow these steps:

- Click on each label, one by one.
- Instead of opening a new Format window, proceed to the top navigation bar and click on the Home tab.
- Utilize the size and font type drop-down fields to enlarge or reduce the axis and legend labels according to your preference.

4.3.4 Modifying the Measurement Options on the Y-axis

To modify the measurement options on the Y-axis in your chart, follow these steps.

- Click on the Y-axis percentages within the chart to launch the Format Axis window. Here, you are allowed to customize how units are displayed on the Axis Options tab. Additionally, you can choose whether to display percentages with no decimal places or two decimal places on the Y-axis.

4.3.5 Finalizing the Creation of Your Graph or Chart

Here are three more steps you can take to enhance your graph:

- Rearrange your data if you want to change the order in which it appears on the graph.
- Add a descriptive title to your graph to clarify its purpose or subject matter.
- Save your chart or graph. After perfecting your graph or chart, you can save it directly as an image file instead of capturing a screenshot within your Excel worksheet. This allows you to obtain a clear picture of the chart that you just created, which you can easily insert into documents, presentations, or other visual materials. To save your chart or graph as an image, simply right-click on the chart or graph and choose the "Save as Picture" option.

4.4 How to Select the Correct Type of Chart for Your Data

At times, you may find yourself in situations where choosing the right chart for your data becomes a challenge. This guide will assist you in identifying the most suitable chart for your specific data.

4.4.1 Excel Data Composition Charts

When you need to display the proportions of a whole, consider using a composition chart. These types of charts are useful for illustrating the sales percentage attributed to every salesperson, website visits categorized by location, or the contribution of every division to the overall revenue.

To represent components of a whole, consider utilizing one of the following types of charts:

- Doughnut: Suitable for multiple data series, each associated with a larger quantity.
- Pie: Ideal for a single data series where the entire sum equals 100 percent.
- Line, bar, column, or stacked: Effective for illustrating components of a whole that evolve over time.

4.4.2 Excel Data Comparison Charts

When you aim to compare different sets of data, you have the option of choosing from several types of charts that are available in Excel. The choice may depend on the hierarchical structure of your information or the number of data sets. For instance, you have the option to compare performance across categories in an employee review or income from different sources.

When presenting comparisons, consider employing one of these chart types:

- Treemap: Ideal for illustrating hierarchical comparisons using rectangles.
- Bar or Column: Effective for showcasing relational differences between categories with two or more data points.
- Scatter: Suitable for data sets involving measurements, requiring a minimum of two sets.
- Sunburst: Appropriate for hierarchical comparisons depicted through rings.
- Bubble: Recommended for scenarios with a minimum of 3 data sets, where the third set will determine the size of the bubble.

4.4.3 Excel Data Trend Charts

When we talk about trends, we're referring to changes that occur over time. Take jeans, for example; their styles have evolved over the decades. In the seventies, we saw bell-bottoms, followed by high-waisted jeans in the eighties, button-fly styles in the nineties, and so forth.

To showcase data that evolves over time, there are several chart types you can utilize:

- Area: Opt for this in lieu of a line chart to highlight the extent of change across time periods.
- Line: Use this with numerous data points to illustrate trends over a period of time, such as years, months, days, or similar intervals, or by category.
- Bar or Column: Employ these to illustrate values across time intervals.

4.4.4 Excel Data Distribution Charts

If you would like to illustrate the breakdown of a substantial dataset, consider employing a distribution chart. This chart type is effective for showcasing test scores across various schools, the occurrence of dissatisfaction in a call center, or survey outcomes categorized by age.

To illustrate the distribution of data, consider these chart types:

- Pareto: Utilize it to reveal the proportion of every category with respect to the total, highlighting significant factors.
- Histogram: Employ this to display the recurrence of values grouped into bins.
- Box and Whisker: Opt for this to depict variations in several sets of data and their connections, using median, quartiles, maximum, and minimum values.
- Scatter: Choose this to showcase connections between different sets of data.

4.4.5 Recommended Charts for One-Off Circumstances

In Excel, there are several other charts that serve specific purposes and may suit your data:

- Funnel: Ideal for illustrating stages in a process that decrease over time.
- Waterfall: Useful for depicting both the negative and positive impacts on values.
- Radar: Great for showcasing values relative to a central point.

- Surface: Handy for visualizing relationships or trends in values across multiple dimensions.

4.5 Managing Your Charts

Here's a guide on how to manage your charts effectively:

4.5.1 Resizing Your Chart

In Excel, resizing charts is a simple task. Follow these steps to resize your chart:

- Click on the chart to select it.
- You'll notice eight points along the border of the chart. Click and drag any of these points to resize the chart as per your requirements.

Note: The text within the chart will remain unchanged while you resize.

4.5.2 Moving Excel Charts

Moving Excel charts within your worksheet is straightforward. Follow these simple steps:

- Click on the chart to select it. When selected, the chart's borders will be highlighted.
- Drag the chart to the desired location within the spreadsheet.

4.5.3 How to Change Your Chart Title

By default, Excel assigns the title "Chart Title" to your chart, which isn't very descriptive. It's essential to have a title that accurately reflects the content of your chart.

Here's how to change the chart title:

- Double-click on the chart to open a menu on the right side of your screen.
- Look for the text "Chart Title" in the menu and edit it to reflect the content of your chart. Once you've made the changes, the title will update accordingly.

Please bear in mind that if you would like to get rid of the chart title entirely, simply click on it and press the Delete button on your keyboard.

4.6 Displaying Data Trends with Sparklines

A sparkline is a small chart embedded within a cell in an Excel worksheet, offering a visual snapshot of data trends. These miniature graphs are handy for illustrating patterns in a value series, like economic trends, seasonal fluctuations, or highlighting peak and low points. For the most effective presentation, place the sparkline close to its corresponding data.

4.6.1 Adding a Sparkline

To add a sparkline, follow these steps:

- Choose an empty cell at the bottom of a data row.
- Click on Insert and choose the type of sparkline, such as column or line.
- Highlight the cells in the row and click the OK option in the menu.
- Need more data rows? Drag the handle to include a sparkline for every row.

4.6.2 Formatting a Sparkline Chart

To format a Sparkline chart, follow these steps:

- Click on the sparkline chart you want to format.
- Go to the Sparkline tab and choose an option:

a) Choose Column, Line, or Win/Loss to alter the type of chart.

b) Enable markers to emphasize single values in your Sparkline chart.

c) Choose a preferred style for your sparkline.

d) Click on Sparkline Color and choose a color.

e) Click on Sparkline Color and click on Weight to select the Sparkline width.

f) Click on Marker Color to modify and pick new marker colors.

g) If you have data that contains negative and positive values, toggle Axis to display the axis.

4.7 Best Practices for Data Visualization

To create effective visualizations, it's essential to adhere to certain principles that ensure clarity and usefulness. These principles enable users to extract valuable insights and make informed decisions based on the data presented without distortion.

Here are some of the best practices when working with data visualization in Excel:

Information richness: Aim for data density to provide sufficient information without overwhelming the viewer. Think of maps—though seemingly simple, they contain vast amounts of data, aiding navigation from one point to another.

Insightfulness: Visualizations should uncover insights that may not be immediately apparent in raw data. They should address the concerns and interests of the audience, offering valuable perspectives.

Familiarity: Opt for familiar chart types over overly creative ones. Select the appropriate chart style based on the type of information you want to convey. For instance, use bar charts to highlight individual values and line charts to emphasize trends.

Clean and Honest: Avoid obscuring the truth with excessive customization options. The goal is to present data truthfully, allowing viewers to draw their own conclusions rather than manipulating them toward a predetermined interpretation.

Consistency: Consistency reinforces familiarity. Using the same visualizations consistently for the same data ensures that users can easily recognize and understand them, facilitating quicker comprehension of key points.

Chapter 5: Intermediate Features and Functions

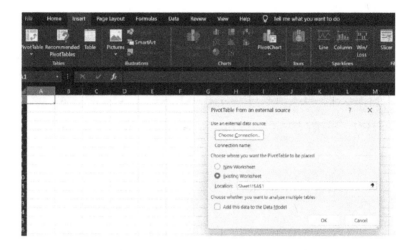

Now, let's delve into the more advanced features and functions of Excel that become valuable as our familiarity with the software grows.

5.1 Lookup Functions in Excel

In this section, we will explore a few of Excel's lookup functions, like Hlookup, Match, and Index:

5.1.1 Hlookup Function

The Hlookup formula in Excel is designed to search for and fetch data from a designated row within a table. The "H" denotes "horizontal," meaning it looks for values in the initial row of your table, progressing horizontally to the right side. Hlookup can perform both exact and approximate matching searches.

The syntax for the HLOOKUP function is as follows:

=HLOOKUP(value, table, row_index, [range_lookup])

Here:

- "value" represents the search key or value you want to find.
- "table" refers to the range of cells containing the data.
- "row_index" indicates the row number in the table from which you want to retrieve the data.
- "[range_lookup]" specifies whether the search should be approximate (true) or exact (false). If omitted, it defaults to true, meaning approximate matching.

5.1.2 Index Function

The index function in Excel is remarkably versatile and robust, making frequent appearances in various advanced formulas. But what's the essence of INDEX? In simple terms, INDEX fetches values from a specified location within a table or list.

The formula structure for INDEX is as follows:

=INDEX(array, row_num, column_num)

5.1.3 Match Function

The MATCH formula serves a singular purpose: determining the numerical position of an item within a list.

The formula structure for MATCH is as follows:

=MATCH(lookup_value, lookup_array, match_type)

5.1.4 Merging the Match and Index Functions

The match and index functions work in harmony to provide more flexibility in adjusting the column index number and row index number dynamically. This dynamic approach helps minimize errors and enhances the efficiency of your index formulas.

The combined formula looks like this:

$$=INDEX(array, MATCH(lookup\_value, lookup\_array, match\_type), MATCH(lookup\_value, lookup\_array, match\_type))$$

5.2 An Introduction to Pivot Tables

A pivot table stands out as one of Excel's most valuable tools for analyzing data. It offers an interactive method to rearrange, examine, and summarize data effectively. With just a few clicks, pivot tables empower users to uncover essential patterns, trends, and insights that might otherwise remain concealed within the dataset.

5.2.1 What Potential Uses Do Pivot Tables Serve?

Pivot tables offer a flexible way to understand and analyze data. They allow you to:

- Summarize and consolidate data: Pivot tables help in calculating counts, averages, totals, and other aggregate functions.

- Sort and filter data: You can easily sort and filter data within pivot tables, focusing on certain subsets as needed.
- Analyze and Compare data: Pivot tables enable analysis of relationships between variables, identification of trends, and comparison of different data points.

5.2.2 Creating a Pivot Table in Microsoft Excel

Making a pivot table in Excel is pretty simple. Here's a quick guide on how to do it:

- First, make sure your data is well organized. It should be arranged neatly in columns and rows, with clear labels at the top of each column. Also, ensure there are no empty columns or rows messing up your data.
- Choose your data by clicking anywhere inside the dataset. Excel will identify the range automatically, but you can also select it manually if required.
- To add a pivot table, navigate to the "Insert" tab located on the Excel ribbon.
- Click on "PivotTable," located in the "Tables" group. This action will prompt a dialog box to appear on your screen.
- Select the range of data you want to include for your pivot table. Excel will suggest a range based on your current selection. If the suggested range is accurate,

you can proceed by clicking "OK." Otherwise, you can manually adjust the range to ensure it includes all the necessary data.

- Decide where you would like your pivot table to appear; you can either create it in a new worksheet or place it within an existing one.
- Configure your pivot table layout: After you've chosen your preferences, Excel will generate a blank pivot table and showcase the PivotTable Field List pane for your convenience.
- Place the fields you wish to analyze into the Filters, Values, Columns, or Rows area of the pivot table by dragging them from the list of column headings in the PivotTable Field List pane.
- Tailor your pivot table to meet your specific needs by adjusting settings such as adding subtotals, formatting cells, and applying filters to concentrate on particular data points.
- If there are any updates to your original data, you can ensure your pivot table reflects those changes by refreshing it. Simply right-click on the pivot table and choose "Refresh" from the options.

5.3 Advanced Conditional Formatting Methods

Conditional formatting stands out as a highly sought-after Microsoft Excel feature, enhancing your spreadsheet by drawing attention to critical elements. This tool empowers data analysts to format cells dynamically or showcase icons based on how well cell values align with predefined rules.

In this section, we'll delve into the application of conditional formatting rules for both numerical and text values. Additionally, we'll explore the functionalities of icon sets and data bars in conditional formatting.

5.3.1 An Overview

Excel is a robust tool that empowers users to arrange, analyze, and showcase data in diverse formats. Among its notable features is conditional formatting, a function that lets users emphasize specific data according to predefined criteria. While many individuals grasp the fundamentals of conditional formatting, there are several advanced methods that can elevate your data presentation. This article delves into these techniques, offering insights on optimizing conditional formatting in Excel for enhanced data visualization.

5.3.2 Emphasizing Values in Cells

Conditional formatting is a widely used technique to emphasize cell values depending on their numeric conditions. For instance, you might want to highlight cells less than or greater than a certain value.

5.3.2.1 How to Highlight Cell Values

- To achieve this, simply choose the cell range,
- Navigate to the "Home" tab,
- Access "Conditional Formatting" and opt for the rule that suits your criteria.

This functionality proves handy in spotting particular data ranges, outliers, or trends.

5.3.3 Icon Sets, Color Scales, and Data Bars

Aside from basic highlighting, Excel provides various pre-set formats accessible through conditional formatting. These formats include icon sets, color scales, and data bars, each offering visual cues to illustrate data differences and patterns. Icon sets, like symbols or arrows, offer quick insights into relative trends or values; color scales use gradients to depict data ranges; and data bars represent values with horizontal bars.

5.3.3.1 How to Add Icon Sets, Color Scales, and Data Bars in Excel

In Excel, adding icon sets, color scales, and data bars can enhance the visual representation of your data. Here's how to apply these formatting options:

- Select Your Data: Begin by selecting the cells or range of cells containing the data you want to format.

- Access Conditional Formatting: Look for the "Conditional Formatting" option under the "Home" tab on the Excel ribbon. Click on it to reveal a drop-down menu.

- Choose Formatting Type: From the drop-down menu, select the type of formatting you want to apply: icon sets, color scales, or data bars.

- Select Formatting Style: Once you've chosen the formatting type, you'll see various styles to choose from. Click on the style that best suits your data visualization needs.

- Customize Formatting (Optional): Excel allows you to customize the formatting options further. You can adjust the thresholds for color scales, choose different icons for icon sets, or modify the appearance of data bars.

- Apply the Formatting: After finalizing your formatting choices, click on them to apply them to the selected data range.

- Review and Modify: Take a moment to review the applied formatting to ensure it effectively highlights the data patterns you want to emphasize. If needed, you can always go back and modify the formatting.

5.3.4 Top or Bottom Rules

In Excel, conditional formatting helps you pinpoint the highest or lowest values in a range. This is handy for quickly identifying important data points. It's commonly used in performance evaluations, sales tracking, and financial analysis. With these rules, you can easily highlight the most significant or least significant values in your dataset.

5.4 Array Functions and Formulas

In this segment, we'll delve into the concept of an Excel array formula, covering the correct method of inputting it into your worksheets and exploring the utilization of array functions.

In Excel, array formulas stand out as a potent tool, albeit a challenging one to fully grasp. With the capability to execute numerous calculations and potentially replace a great number of conventional formulas, a single array formula holds substantial power. Surprisingly, a significant portion of users, around 90%, tend to shy away from delving into array functions due to apprehension about the learning curve.

Certainly, array formulas in Excel often pose a significant challenge for learners. However, the objective of this section is to simplify the learning process, ensuring it's as straightforward and manageable as can be.

5.4.1 How Does an Excel Array Work?

Before delving into array formulas and functions, it's essential to grasp the concept of an "array." Fundamentally, an array denotes a grouping of items, which can encompass numbers or text. These items may be organized in a singular column or row, or they may span across multiple columns and rows.

Consider this: Imagine jotting down your weekly grocery needs in an array format in your Excel spreadsheet:

{"Meat", "Rice", "Eggs", "Cheese"}

Now, picture selecting cells C1 through F1, entering the array (preceded by "=") into the formula bar, and hitting CTRL + SHIFT + ENTER. What you've accomplished is crafting a one-dimensional horizontal array. It's not too daunting, is it?

5.4.2 What Does a Microsoft Excel Array Formula Mean?

In Excel, the distinction between a regular formula and an array formula lies in their processing of values. Unlike a regular formula, an array formula can handle multiple values simultaneously. Essentially, it evaluates each value within an array and executes various calculations based on the specified conditions outlined in the formula. This capability allows for more complex and dynamic calculations within Excel spreadsheets.

An array formula isn't just about handling multiple values together; it's also capable of returning numerous values concurrently. In essence, when you use an array formula, the results it gives back are also presented as an array. This means you can process multiple data points and obtain corresponding outputs all at once, making it a powerful tool for advanced calculations in Excel.

Array formulas are supported across various versions of Excel, including 2007, 2010, 2013, 2016, 2019, and earlier versions.

5.4.2.1 Basic Excel Array Formula Example

Let's say you have a list of items in column C and their corresponding prices in column D, and you would like to find the overall sales amount.

Instead of calculating subtotals for every row manually, you can use an array formula to streamline the process and save time. Here's how you can do it in two simple steps:

- Choose a blank cell where you would like the result to appear.
- Enter the formula: =SUM(C2:C6*D2:D6) into the cell.
- To finalize the array formula, press CTRL + SHIFT + ENTER.
- Once entered, Excel wraps the formula with {curly braces}, signaling it's an array formula. This method allows you to perform calculations across multiple cells efficiently.

This example illustrates the efficiency of array formulas, especially when dealing with large datasets. By using just one formula, you can perform complex calculations across multiple rows, saving you valuable time and effort.

5.4.3 Dynamic Arrays, Spilling, and Spill Range

Dynamic arrays are like magic spreadsheets that adjust in size and calculate on their own. You enter a formula in one cell, and it magically populates multiple cells with the results.

Over the span of more than three decades, Microsoft Excel has evolved, but the principle of one formula, one cell has endured. In the world of traditional array formulas, each cell requiring a result demanded the input of a formula. Dynamic arrays have changed this age-old rule. Presently, any formula generating an array of values spills seamlessly into adjacent cells, eliminating the need for complex maneuvers like Ctrl + Shift + Enter. In essence, handling dynamic arrays has become as straightforward as dealing with a solitary cell.

Let's delve into a simple example of how dynamic arrays work in Excel.

Imagine you have two columns of numbers in Excel: Column A contains the prices of various items, and Column B contains the corresponding quantities sold. You want to calculate the total revenue for each item by multiplying the price by the quantity sold.

In traditional Excel, you might have to enter a formula in each row to compute the revenue for each item. However, with dynamic arrays, you can streamline this process.

Here's how it works:

- In an empty cell, let's say Cell C1, enter the formula: =A1:A5 * B1:B5.
- Press Enter.

What happens next is where dynamic arrays shine. Instead of getting a single result in Cell C1, you'll notice that Excel automatically populates the adjacent cells below with the calculated revenue for each item. This automatic expansion of results across multiple cells is the essence of dynamic arrays.

So, without needing to enter the formula in each row individually, Excel dynamically computes the revenue for each item based on the corresponding price and quantity sold. This makes managing and analyzing data more efficient and less cumbersome, especially when dealing with large datasets.

When you enter a formula that produces results in multiple adjacent cells, it's known as spilling. The area where these results appear is termed the spill range.

In conclusion, it's crucial to understand that the recent Excel update doesn't merely introduce a different approach to managing arrays; it represents a revolutionary shift in the entire calculation engine. Dynamic arrays bring a set of new functions to the Excel Function Library, enhancing the speed and efficiency of existing ones. The ultimate goal is to phase out the traditional array formulas, entered with the Ctrl + Shift + Enter shortcut, in favor of these dynamic arrays.

5.5 Inserting, Embedding, and Linking Data

In this section, we'll explore ways to enhance your Excel spreadsheet experience. We'll cover inserting objects directly into your spreadsheet, embedding objects within your worksheet, and adding links to files for seamless integration.

You have the option of incorporating content from various programs, like Microsoft Word, into your document using Object Linking and Embedding (OLE).

Many programs support OLE, a system that allows content created in one program to be used in another. For instance, you can place a Microsoft Word document inside a Microsoft Excel workbook.

- To view the content types available for insertion, go to the Insert tab.
- Locate the text group and click on Object.

The Object type box will show only programs installed on your laptop that support OLE objects.

5.5.1 Embedding Objects in a Spreadsheet
Embedding an object in a spreadsheet is straightforward:

- Choose the cell within the worksheet where you would like to embed the object.
- Navigate to the Insert tab and click on Object within the Text group.
- Select the Create from File tab in the dialog box labeled "Object."
- Hit the Browse button and pick the file you would like to insert.

- If you prefer displaying an icon in your worksheet instead of the file contents, check the Display as icon box. If no checkboxes are selected, the Excel program will display the initial page of the file. In either case, double-clicking opens the whole file. Hit the OK button to apply the changes.

Keep in mind: Once you've added the file or icon, feel free to drag and drop it to any location on your worksheet. You also have the option of resizing the file or icon by using the handles for resizing. To locate these handles, simply click the icon or file once.

5.5.2 Adding a File Link

Consider adding a link to your object instead of embedding it entirely. This is feasible if the object you wish to include and the workbook are both housed on a shared network drive, a SharePoint site, or a related location, and if the file locations remain unchanged. Linking is advantageous, especially if the object frequently undergoes updates, because the link will always open the most current version of the embedded document.

Important: If you relocate the linked file to a different location, the link will no longer function.

- Choose the cell within the worksheet where you would like to place the object.
- Navigate to the Insert tab, and select Object in the Text group.
- Select the Create from File tab.
- Choose "Browse" and pick the desired file for linking.
- Check the "Link to file" option, then hit the OK option to apply changes.

5.5.3 How to Create New Objects from Within Excel

Imagine creating a fresh object using a different program, all while staying within your workbook. Picture this: you're working in Excel and wish to enrich your table or chart with a thorough description. Instead of switching applications, you can seamlessly add your document—be it a PowerPoint presentation or a Word document—right into Excel. You have the option to display it directly within your worksheet or include an icon for easy access to the file.

- Start by selecting the cell in the worksheet where you wish to place the object.
- Navigate to the Insert tab and find the Text group. Click on Object.

- Choose the type of object you'd like inserted from the options listed on the Create New tab. Check the Display as icon box if you prefer to add an icon instead of inserting an object.
- Hit OK. Based on the file type, a new program window might open, or an editing window will appear directly within the Excel program.
- Proceed to create the new object you intend to insert.

Once you've completed your task and Excel opens a new program window for creating the object, feel free to carry on your work directly within that window.

After finishing your work, there's no need to save the embedded object separately. Simply close the workbook, and your newly created objects will be automatically saved.

Remember, once you've added the object, you have the flexibility to move it around your Excel worksheet simply by dragging and dropping it. Additionally, if you need to resize the object, just click on it once to reveal the resizing handles, then adjust accordingly.

Chapter 6: Advanced Excel Features

6.1 Co-authoring and Collaborative Editing

For a long time, Excel enthusiasts have had the ability to team up on shared workbooks. This capability, allowing numerous users to collaborate on one file, has opened up numerous avenues for enhancing productivity and efficiency, thanks to Microsoft's initiative.

Thanks to Office 365, there's been a notable shift in the way we handle documents—from merely "sharing" files within the office to actively "co-authoring" them online. While the option to share workbooks in the traditional sense is still there, it's now tucked away by default. Unless you are firmly tied to the old ways of sharing or need specific features only available with shared workbooks, it's wise to embrace the shift. According to Microsoft, the future is all about co-authoring.

If diving into Excel co-authoring is uncharted territory for you, or if teaming up on workbooks is a fresh concept, here are some helpful tips to kickstart your journey (and a heads-up on common pitfalls to steer clear of).

6.1.1 The System of Co-Authoring

While co-authoring within Excel, you and your teammates can collectively contribute to and modify the same workbook simultaneously. Witness each other's cursors in real-time, each uniquely colored, and see edits happening as they unfold.

- To kick off co-authoring with your team in an Excel workbook, you should click the "Share" button located in the top-right corner of the window. If the file is not already stored online, like on OneDrive, you'll receive a prompt to upload a copy.
- Once the file is prepared for sharing, a dialog box will appear on your screen.
- In the top box, you can set the access preferences for the file. The default setting grants editing access to anyone with the link. To reveal additional options, make sure to click on the box. You have the flexibility to limit access to individuals within your company or to certain people. Moreover, you can establish a shared access expiration date, add a

password to the file, and decide if you would like to permit downloading or not.

- Following that, if you wish, you can input contact details and a message. You then have the option to send an email invitation straight from the dialog. As an alternative, you can copy the link or initiate a new message in Outlook, taking charge of sending out the invitations yourself.
- Lastly, if your goal is to share a copy of the file, you can pick the format, such as a PDF or Excel workbook file. Then, Excel conveniently attaches your file to a fresh email message in Outlook.

Note: In newer Excel versions, the version history feature isn't as comprehensive as it used to be when sharing workbooks. Nonetheless, you can still access a list of previously stored versions and revert the file to an earlier one if needed. While this can be a lifesaver in critical situations (just roll back to an earlier version), seasoned Excel users might find the reduced level of detail frustrating.

6.2 Introducing VBA and Macros

In Excel, VBA Macros utilize the Visual Basic Application to craft personalized user-generated functions, making manual tasks more efficient through automated processes. Moreover, VBA extends its capabilities to access the Windows Application Programming Interface (API). A primary application of VBA is in the customization of the user interface, allowing the creation of customized forms, dialog boxes, menus, and toolbars.

6.2.1 Creating VBA Macros in Excel

- To access the VBA window in Excel, simply press Alt+F11. This opens up the platform for users to start coding macros.
- To kick off the coding process, users need to set up a module file, which houses a collection of macros. Hit Insert and click on Module to create a fresh module. If desired, you can assign a name to this module by utilizing the properties window located in the editor's lower-left corner. Just type in the new module name and hit enter.

6.2.2 The Process of Naming VBA Macros

Firstly, it's important to assign a unique name to the macro. This name must be distinct from other macros and typically shouldn't match the names of other tools, functions, or properties in Excel. The macro name is what users will use to activate the macro.

To give a macro its name, users should type "Sub name()" and hit "enter" in the editor's coding window. This action automatically populates the window with the extensive format of a macro in Excel. For instance, if you want to name the macro "Our Macro," simply type "Sub ourMacro()" and hit the enter key. A few lines below the "Sub," the VBA Editor will systematically insert an "End Sub" line.

Keep in mind: When naming variables, functions, or macros in VBA, it's customary to use lowercase for single words and capitalize the first letter of each new word. VBA names typically don't have spaces. Since "Our Macro" is composed of two words, it should be written as "ourMacro." Nevertheless, these are just suggested practices and aren't strictly enforced.

6.2.3 Sub-Names in VBA

In VBA, the "Sub Name()" line marks the beginning of the macro code, while "End Sub" indicates its end. Users can create additional macros by starting a new "Sub Name()" line below the first "End Sub." Excel will inevitably insert a line between the two distinct macros. This represents the fundamental structure of an Excel macro.

6.3 An Introduction to Power Pivot, Power Query, and Power Bi in Excel

For newcomers, distinguishing between the different Power BI tools can feel daunting. Questions arise: What sets Power Query apart from Power Pivot? How does

Power Pivot differ from Power BI? And crucially, when should you opt for one over the other?

In this section, we'll dissect each power tool one at a time, elucidate their roles, and explore how they seamlessly complement each other.

6.3.1 Power Pivot

Power Pivot serves the purpose of modeling your data and executing more intricate calculations beyond the capabilities of Excel.

Power Pivot proves invaluable when handling large datasets. After Power Query finishes importing and refining data from diverse sources, Power Pivot steps in to establish connections between the queries and tables.

Next, with Data Analysis Expressions (DAX), which serves as Power Pivot's formula language, you can craft more robust calculations and intricate data models compared to what Excel alone can offer.

Initially, Power Pivot was only accessible as an add-on, but starting in Excel 2013, it's become a built-in feature of Excel.

- To access Power Pivot, simply proceed to the Data tab and click the Go to the Power Pivot Window button.
- You have the option to proceed to the Ribbon and reveal the Power Pivot tab, which is concealed by default.
- To access customization options for the Ribbon, simply right-click anywhere on the Ribbon and select "Customize the Ribbon."
- Ensure to mark the checkbox next to Power Pivot on the right-side, then click Ok to apply changes.

The Power Pivot tab includes a button for opening the Power Pivot window, similar to the Data tab. It also allows you to create measures (using the DAX formula) straight from within Excel, along with a few additional features.

The Power Pivot window offers two views. The Data view resembles Excel, allowing you to visualize your data and craft columns that are calculated and measured with the use of DAX formulas. The diagram view, on the other hand, is where you create connections between your tables.

Once your model is prepared, you can delve into the analysis and reporting of your data with the use of pivot tables.

6.3.2 Power Query

In Excel, Power Query serves as the go-to instrument for importing, refining, and organizing data.

Initially introduced in Excel 2013, Power Query came as an add-on called Power Query. However, starting from Excel 2016 and in Microsoft 365, it can be accessed directly within Excel from the Data tab, although it is now known as Get & Transform.

Power Query can bring in data from diverse sources like Salesforce, Facebook, folders on drives, text files, and CSVs. It's regularly updated with new connections, simplifying the process of fetching data from external sources.

Once you import data, which involves connecting to a source, the Power Query Editor window will open up for you.

This tool packs a punch, offering immense power and remarkable usefulness, all while maintaining simplicity in its usage. Its user-friendly interface features a range of commands that will feel familiar to many Excel users.

When users execute commands to tidy and refine their data, like removing duplicates, replacing values, or splitting columns, Power Query logs each step and generates M code in the background, akin to how VBA is generated when recording a macro.

M serves as the language in Power Query, distinguishing itself from Excel formulas and requiring a bit of finesse to grasp. Power Query keeps the code discreet by concealing the Formula Bar, though you can reveal it in the Power Query Editor by clicking View and selecting Formula Bar.

For those well-versed in Power Query, tweaking the code is possible through the Home tab's Advanced Editor or straight from within the Formula Bar. The actions taken by a user are documented in the Applied Steps pane, offering a space to delete, edit, or view those steps. It's worth noting that Power Query doesn't boast an undo button; removing a step essentially serves as its undo mechanism.

Every single one of these actions gets stored in the query. To prepare the query for analysis, you can click on Home to load it, followed by clicking the list arrow on the "Close and Load" button, and next selecting "Close and Load To."

You have the option to load your data directly into a table within Excel, integrate it into a pivot table, or simply establish it as a connection.

When you load the data directly into a pivot table, you sidestep the physical constraints and hassle that Excel may encounter. This approach helps prevent unwieldy file sizes since the data isn't stored directly within Excel.

Opting for loading as a connection allows you to handle more substantial datasets, surpassing Excel's capacity of over one million rows, without burdening your file sizes since the data isn't stored directly in Excel. This approach also opens the door for more advanced calculations through Power Pivot.

You can rerun queries at a later date by proceeding to the Data tab and hitting the Refresh button or utilizing Excel's Queries and Connections pane.

Consider the possibilities for routine data imports and reports you might generate. The entire process can be simplified by just clicking the refresh button.

6.3.3 Power BI

Power BI refers to two distinct tools: Power BI Service (also known as PowerBI.com) and Power BI Desktop.

You can explore Power BI at no cost by signing up for a free Microsoft Fabric account, which serves as an all-in-one analytics platform for data professionals and businesses. If you're using it individually, you only require the free desktop app and a complimentary Fabric license for publishing your reports on the workspace.

Yet, when it comes to sharing your content with other people, a paid subscription is necessary. This could be either the PPU (Power BI Premium Per User) or Power BI Pro option. Both PPU licenses and paid Fabric licenses grant companies access to the premium features offered by Power BI.

This tool employs the Power Pivot and Power Query engines to fetch, clean, and model your data, preparing it for reporting. Therefore, the skills you acquire for these tools in Excel seamlessly apply to Power BI Desktop as well.

Power BI offers advantages over standard Excel, particularly in how data is visualized. Visualizing data encompasses matrixes, tables, slicers, and charts that you can integrate into your Power BI reports.

Power BI offers a wider array of visualizations compared to Excel. Moreover, it provides numerous options for how these visualizations interrelate with each other on a page or even throughout the whole report.

This list of visualizations is continuously expanding, with the option to download more from the marketplace and the opportunity to craft your own personalized visuals.

Power BI Desktop serves as the space for constructing your model, executing DAX calculations, and crafting your reports. Subsequently, you can publish these creations on PowerBI.com.

Once your reports are published, others can access and engage with them on PowerBI.com. This accessibility extends to any mobile device or web browser.

Additionally, you can generate dashboards using the PowerBI.com service to highlight key insights from your reports. Moreover, you have the option to refresh any reports that have been shared with you.

6.3.4 What Is the Combined Effect of These Tools?

You don't necessarily have to use both Power Pivot and Power Query together. They function independently, so you might find that one or the other suffices for your needs.

Power Query can handle the preparation of sizable yet straightforward datasets for analysis. On the other hand, Power Pivot steps in for more intricate models and robust calculations beyond the capabilities of Excel PivotTables or worksheet functions alone.

While these two tools are capable of standalone use, they complement each other quite well. Power Pivot includes features for shaping and importing data, but it's advisable to let Power Query handle these tasks.

Once the data is imported, it's loaded into the Power Pivot model to start forming connections and crafting measures with DAX.

Power BI is a distinct tool encompassing both Power Query and Power Pivot functionalities. It boasts a broader range of connection alternatives compared to Excel's Power Query. Additionally, Power BI offers superior visualizations and facilitates enhanced sharing of reports through integration with the Power BI Service.

Power BI might feel a bit like using a hammer to smash your fruit, whereas Excel is the tool that most people are familiar with and genuinely appreciate.

There are advantages to speaking the language of people by utilizing the simple Excel tools, unless you specifically need

the enhanced visuals and additional capabilities offered by
Power BI.

Chapter 7: Optimizing Your Workflow with Shortcuts

7.1 Introduction to Keyboard Shortcuts

In Excel, numerous keyboard shortcuts are available to boost productivity and enhance your efficiency. Rather than relying on the mouse to navigate the toolbar, you can achieve remarkable functions with just 2–3 keystrokes. Doesn't that make things simpler and save time? Utilizing these keyboard shortcuts significantly accelerates your work pace, ultimately reducing the overall time spent on tasks.

The question at hand is whether you need to commit these shortcuts to memory. The answer is no; it's not a necessity. Yet, having a grasp of a few of them can be advantageous. Through consistent practice, you'll find that recalling the most common keyboard shortcuts for Excel becomes second nature.

Now, let's delve into the cheat sheet for keyboard shortcuts, a handy reference for your work in Excel. Here, I've organized a few Excel shortcuts according to their functions. To begin, let's explore the shortcut keys related to workbook operations.

7.2 Workbook Keyboard Shortcuts

In this part, we'll cover the fundamental operations of working with a workbook. You'll discover how to start a new workbook, access an existing one, and save your spreadsheet to prevent any loss of data or calculations. Additionally, we'll explore how you can navigate between multiple sheets within a workbook.

1. To access an already existing workbook, just press Ctrl + O.
2. To start a new workbook, simply press Ctrl + N.
3. If you'd like to close the workbook you are currently working on, use Ctrl + W.
4. To save your spreadsheet or workbook, use the shortcut Ctrl + S.
5. To switch to the previous Excel sheet, use the shortcut Ctrl + PageUp.
6. Navigate to the next Excel sheet by simply pressing Ctrl + PageDown on your keyboard.
7. To exit Excel, use the keyboard shortcut Ctrl + F4.
8. To access the View tab in Excel, simply press Alt + W.
9. To navigate to the Data tab in Excel, press Alt + A.
10. To access the Formula tab in Excel, use the shortcut Alt + M.

7.3 Cell Formatting Keyboard Shortcuts

In Excel, each cell contains the data you're working with. You can perform various actions on cells using shortcuts, like editing content, aligning text, adding borders, creating outlines, and more. Let's take a quick look at some of these keyboard shortcuts.

1. To modify a cell's content, press F2.
2. To italicize text, use Ctrl + I, and to make the font bold, use Ctrl + B.

3. To copy cells, press Ctrl + C, and to paste them, press Ctrl + V.
4. To fill color, press the Alt + H + H keys on your keyboard.
5. To center-align your cell content, use Alt + H + A + C.
6. When you want to get rid of that outline border, hit Ctrl + Shift + _.
7. If you'd like to add a border, use the Alt + H + B keys on your keyboard.
8. To go back to the previous cell, press the Shift + Tab keys on your keyboard.
9. To jump to the next cell, simply hit the Tab key.
10. If you want to put an outline around select cells, just press Ctrl + Shift + &.
11. To choose every cell on the left side, simply hold down Ctrl + Shift + Left Arrow.
12. If you want to choose every cell on the right side, just press Ctrl + Shift + Right arrow.
13. If you'd like to choose every cell below the chosen cell, hold down the Ctrl + Shift + Down Arrow keys on your keyboard.
14. If you want to choose every cell above the chosen one, just press Ctrl + Shift + Up Arrow.
15. To choose the entire column from your selected cell to the table's end, hold down Ctrl + Shift + Down Arrow on your keyboard.

7.4 Advanced Cell Formatting Keyboard Shortcuts

Besides the cell formatting shortcuts mentioned earlier, let's explore a few additional and advanced Excel shortcuts for cell formatting that could be quite useful.

1. To remove a cell comment, hit the Shift + F10 + D keys.
2. To insert a comment into a cell, press Shift + F2.
3. To turn on the filter, use either Alt + Down Arrow or Ctrl + Shift + L.
4. To open the find and replace feature, press Ctrl + H.
5. If you would like to add the current time, hold the Ctrl + Shift + : keys on your keyboard.
6. To input the current date, press Ctrl + ;.
7. To format as a percentage, use the Ctrl + Shift + % keys on your keyboard.
8. To format as currency, hit the Ctrl + Shift + $ keys.
9. If you want to create a hyperlink, press Ctrl+K.
10. If you would like to access the "Tell me what you want to do" box, press the Alt + Q keys.

7.5 Column and Row Formatting Keyboard Shortcuts

Here, we'll explore essential shortcuts for formatting columns and rows. We'll cover deleting and hiding columns and rows as well as grouping and ungrouping them.

1. If you want to choose the whole column, hold down the Ctrl + Space keys.
2. To choose the whole row, press Shift + Space.
3. To get rid of a row, first select the entire row using Shift + Space, then press Ctrl + -.
4. To remove a column, use Alt + H + D + C.
5. To conceal a chosen column, press Ctrl + 0.
6. To reveal a hidden column, use Ctrl + Shift + 0.
7. To conceal a chosen row, hit Ctrl + 9.
8. To reveal a hidden row, press Ctrl + Shift + 9.
9. If you would like to create a group of columns or rows, press the Alt + Shift + Right arrow keys on your keyboard.
10. To separate previously grouped columns or rows, press Alt + Shift + Left arrow.

7.6 Pivot Table Formatting Keyboard Shortcuts

Let's dive into key shortcuts for formatting pivot tables in this section.

1. To conceal items in a pivot table, simply use Ctrl + -.
2. To group items in a pivot table, simply use Alt + Shift + Right arrow.
3. To break apart grouped items in a pivot table, just press Alt + Shift + Left arrow.

4. To craft a pivot chart on a fresh worksheet, simply press F11.
5. If you want to generate a pivot chart on the very same sheet, press the Alt + F1 keys on your keyboard.

Conclusion

In wrapping up our journey through the basics of Excel for beginners, let's distill the key takeaways. Excel, a versatile tool, empowers users to organize and analyze data with ease. We've touched on fundamental functions, from basic formulas to sorting and filtering data. It's a dynamic canvas where you can structure information intuitively.

As you navigate through Excel's interface, the ribbon becomes your ally, housing a range of tools to format and visualize data. Embracing keyboard shortcuts, like Ctrl + C and Ctrl + V, accelerates your workflow. Remember, Excel is more than just rows and columns; it's a canvas where numbers transform into insights.

Whether you're creating a simple budget or diving into complex data analysis, Excel adapts to your needs. The newfound ability to create different charts provides a visual dimension to your data story. Experiment, explore, and let Excel be your companion on this data-driven journey.

In conclusion, mastering Excel for beginners is about fostering familiarity and confidence. Take these foundational steps, and you'll find yourself equipped to tackle various tasks efficiently. Excel is not just a spreadsheet program; it's a gateway to unraveling the potential within your data. So, armed with these insights, go forth and let Excel be your canvas for data exploration and decision-making.

END

Thank you for reading my book.

Robert B. Klatt

www.ingramcontent.com/pod-product-compliance
Lightning Source LLC
LaVergne TN
LVHW051246050326
832903LV00028B/2590